T·E·R·R·O·R·I·S·M

THE HISTORY OF
TERRORISM

By Don Nardo

Content Adviser: Jarret Brachman, Ph.D.,
author of *Global Jihadism: Theory and Practice*
and senior U.S. government counterterrorism consultant

Reading Adviser: Alexa L. Sandmann, Ed.D., Professor of Literacy,
College and Graduate School of Education, Health, and Human Services,
Kent State University

COMPASS POINT BOOKS
a capstone imprint

Compass Point Books
151 Good Counsel Drive
P.O. Box 669
Mankato, MN 56002-0669

Editor: Brenda Haugen
Designer: Heidi Thompson
Media Researcher: Eric Gohl
Library Consultant: Kathleen Baxter
Production Specialist: Jane Klenk

Image Credits: akg-images/Peter Connolly, 11; Alamy/North Wind Picture Archives,
24; AP Images, 40; AP Images/David J. Phillip, 41; Art Resource, N.Y./Bildarchiv
Preussischer Kulturbesitz, 27; Art Resource, N.Y./Erich Lessing, 9; Corbis/Bettmann,
22; Corbis/Hulton-Deutsch Collection, 39; Getty Images Inc./AFP, 28, 31, 33; Getty
Images Inc./AFP/Paul J. Richards, 4; Getty Images Inc./Dean Purcell, 43; Getty
Images Inc./Hulton Archive, 19; Getty Images Inc./Imagno, 7; Getty Images Inc./
Kaveh Kazemi, cover; Getty Images Inc./Nadar, 25; Getty Images Inc./Warrick Page,
12; Library of Congress, 35, 36; Mary Evans Picture Library, 14, 16; The Bridgeman
Art Library/Peter Newark Pictures/Private Collection, 20.

This book was manufactured with paper containing
at least 10 percent post-consumer waste.

Library of Congress Cataloging-in-Publication Data
Nardo, Don, 1947–
  The history of terrorism / by Don Nardo.
    p. cm.
Includes bibliographical references and index.
ISBN 978-0-7565-4310-5 (library binding)
1. Terrorism—History—Juvenile literature. 2. Terrorism—
History—United States—Juvenile literature. I. Title.
HV6431.N3656 2010
363.32509—dc22   2009026279

Visit Compass Point Books on the Internet at *www.compasspointbooks.com*
or e-mail your request to *custserv@compasspointbooks.com*

TABLE OF CONTENTS ////////////

A DEADLY EXAMPLE FOR LATER AGES /////////

In 2001 U.S. President George W. Bush announced the start of what came to be called the war on terror. Speaking to Congress in September, he said: "Our enemy is a radical network of terrorists and every government that supports them." He added that the war on terror "will not end until every terrorist group of global reach has been found, stopped, and defeated."

Bush's impassioned speech was a reaction to one of the most shocking events in modern times. Nine days earlier, on September 11, 2001, the United States had come under attack. Islamic extremists belonging to a group calling itself al-Qaida hijacked four commercial airliners. They crashed two of them into the

President George W. Bush met with rescue workers at Ground Zero after the September 11, 2001, attacks.

World Trade Center towers in New York City. Another plane struck the Pentagon building near Washington, D.C. The fourth crashed in a field in Pennsylvania after brave passengers thwarted the hijackers' plans to hit other targets in Washington.

Trying to Define Terrorism

This was not the first time al-Qaida had struck American targets. Nor is al-Qaida the first terrorist organization to use violence. Terrorism is not even new to modern times. Evidence shows that terrorists have existed throughout recorded history.

Not all of these individuals and groups saw themselves as terrorists, however. Often they claimed that their violent tactics were justified. They defined terrorism one way, while their victims defined it another. As a result, dozens of definitions for terrorism have emerged over the years.

A good example of how hard it is to define terrorism can be seen in the way the word entered the English language. *Terror* comes from the Latin word *terrere*, meaning "to frighten." It first appeared in English-language dictionaries in 1798. The French Revolution was still going on. The French people's bloody struggle to overthrow France's corrupt monarchy had begun in 1789. At first demands for justice and equality were the rebels' rallying cries. But between September 1793 and July 1794, extremists took control of the revolution. This period became known as the Reign of Terror. Justifying the use of fear and violence, one of its leaders, Maximilien Robespierre, said: "Terror is nothing other than justice, prompt, severe, inflexible."

King Louis XVI of France was beheaded
by guillotine during the French Revolution.

In the name of democracy, 300,000 people were arrested during the Reign of Terror. About 17,000 were tried and executed. Another 12,000 were executed without a trial. Thousands more died in jail. Later generations came to see that period as a time of injustice rather than justice. In general, rational, peace-loving people came to see terrorism as a bad thing under any circumstances.

Today a terrorist is commonly described as someone who commits extreme acts to create fear. These acts often include bombings, murders, and kidnappings. While terrorists' motives differ, they usually hope fear will persuade their victims to meet their demands.

Terror as a National Policy

No one knows who the first terrorists were. When and where they existed is also a mystery. The first written references to the use of terrorist acts date back about 2,800 years. They appear in the official records of the kings of ancient Assyria. At the time, the Assyrians were building an empire in Mesopotamia. This was the ancient name for the region today

Proud of His Cruelty

Assyria's King Assurnasirpal II saw nothing wrong with committing cruel acts during his conquests. He bragged about these acts: "Many [of the defeated] I took as living captives. From some I cut off their hands and their fingers, and from others I cut off their noses, their ears, and their fingers, [and] of many I put out the eyes. I made one [pile] of the living, and another of heads, and I bound their heads to posts round about the city. Their young men and maidens I burned in the fire."

occupied by Iraq.

The Assyrian kings ordered what are now seen as terrorist acts as part of their national policy. Today the term for this is "state-sponsored terrorism." Among the modern countries that have been accused of sponsoring terrorist acts at one time or another are Libya, Iran,

Victorious Assyrian warriors often returned home carrying the heads of their enemies.

and Iraq. However, these acts pale in comparison with the horrifying crimes committed by Assyria's monarchs.

One of them was King Assurnasirpal II, who reigned from about 883 B.C. to 859 B.C. Like other Assyrian kings, he used extreme violence and fear as a means of control. On his orders, his soldiers brutalized and terrorized newly conquered peoples. The goal was to make them, as well as other Assyrian subjects, afraid to complain or rebel.

The "Dagger Men"

Other ancient terrorists took a different approach, becoming almost invisible in their terror. They formed small groups dedicated to fighting national governments and others in power. Often they employed terror tactics against foreign conquerors who were occupying their lands.

The earliest recorded terrorists of this kind were called *sicarii*—"dagger men." They lived in Palestine in the first century A.D. Then called Judea, the area had become a province of the Roman Empire. Most Jews in Judea despised Roman rule. Sometime in the 50s, the most extreme of their number, the sicarii, emerged. In their view, some Jewish leaders were too friendly with the Roman occupiers. So the group targeted prominent Jews as well as Romans. The first-century Jewish historian Josephus described their methods: "Their favorite trick was to mingle with festival crowds, concealing under their garments small daggers with which they stabbed their opponents. When their victims fell, the assassins melted into the [crowd]. More terrible than the

Among the crowds at festivals in ancient Jerusalem's marketplace lurked dagger men carrying concealed weapons.

crimes themselves was the fear they aroused, everyman hourly expecting death, as in war."

Thus both the Assyrian rulers and the sicarii became very skilled at using fear as a weapon. Through history many other individuals and groups would follow their deadly example.

USING ASSASSINATION AS A TOOL //////////////////////

The sicarii used murder to achieve their political aims. Several later terrorist organizations used that technique even more effectively. The most famous of them—the Assassins—thrived in medieval times. The medieval era, sometimes called the Middle Ages, began after the fall of Rome in the late 400s and lasted about 1,000 years.

The Assassins were such expert killers that they struck fear into the hearts of people over many generations. As a result, their name outlived them. The modern terms *assassin* and *assassination* come from it. Today an assassin is someone who kills, or tries to kill, a well-known person. This is exactly what

Benazir Bhutto, Pakistan's first and only female prime minister, was assassinated in December 2007.

the medieval Assassins did. They murdered well-known religious, military, and political leaders. That approach spread fear, giving the Assassins some control over society.

The Eagle's Nest

Like some modern terrorist groups, the Assassins were based in the Middle East. In early medieval times, a new religion—Islam—spread through that region. Most members of the

Daggers were one of the earliest weapons. With its double-edged blade, a dagger can be used for stabbing or cutting.

faith, called Muslims, were moderate in their religious and political views. Those in a few small groups that splintered from the main group were more extreme. They came to hate the Muslim rulers of most Middle Eastern kingdoms and cities. The extremists thought the rulers were greedy and unjust. They also accused the rulers of not taking certain basic religious principles seriously enough.

In the late 11th century, one such extremist group decided to take action. Its goal became to forcibly remove some caliphs, sultans, and other rulers from power. Being few in number and having no army, the group created a secret organization of killers. This marked the birth of the Hashshashin, better known as the Assassins.

Soon the group was active across what are now Iraq, Iran, and Syria. The Assassins built secret strongholds

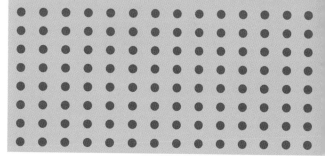

Imposing Mountain Stronghold

The Eagle's Nest was in an isolated highland region in northern Iran. An imposing stone fortress, it was perched on top of a cliff more than 6,000 feet (1,830 meters) high. The hideout could be reached only by one very steep path. That made it easy to defend against approaching enemies.

where they lived and trained. Usually they were in remote areas in the mountains. That made it difficult for soldiers to find them. The most famous of the fortresses was the Alamut ("Eagle's Nest").

Assassins' Rules and Weapons

The remoteness of the Assassins' hideouts was not the only reason for their success. Another was that the Assassins were highly organized. The group's supreme leader bore the title grand master. His authority was unquestioned. Stories claim that his followers would willingly leap off cliffs to their deaths if he told them to. The grand master's assistants were called grand priors. Each grand prior commanded a cell, a subgroup of Assassins. Many modern terrorist groups use the idea of division into cells. Below

The leader of the Assassins sometimes showed his power over his group members by ordering them to kill themselves.

Structure of Assassins

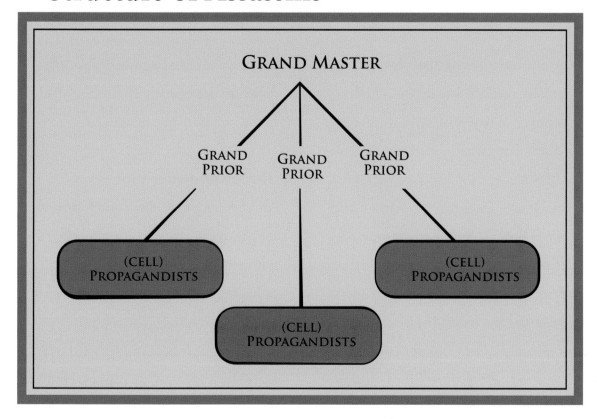

the priors were the other members of the Assassins, known as the propagandists. They carried out murders and other activities ordered by the grand master and grand priors.

In committing their political murders, the Assassins followed strict guidelines. These were likely created by the first grand master, Hassan-i-Sabbah, or his immediate successors. According to Bernard Lewis, an expert on the Assassins, "Their weapon was almost always the same—the dagger, wielded by the appointed Assassin in person. It is significant that they made virtually no use of such safer weapons as were available to them at the time—the bow and crossbow, missiles [spears], and poison. [The] Assassin himself, having struck down the assigned victim, made no attempt to escape, nor was any attempt made to rescue him. On the contrary, to have survived a mission was seen as a disgrace."

Following these rules, the Assassins struck time and again with devastating effect. In 1092 they murdered the ruler of Baghdad, Nizam al-Mulk. In the years that followed, they eliminated many other Muslim leaders. The Assassins also sometimes killed Christian leaders who came to Palestine during the Crusades. The Crusades were wars fought between Muslims and Christians over possession of holy sites in the region.

For nearly two centuries, the Assassins seemed almost invincible. But they were unable either to frighten or defend against the Mongols. Savage warriors from central Asia, the Mongols conquered the Middle East in the 1250s. They assaulted and destroyed all of the Assassins' fortresses, including

the Eagle's Nest. The once influential Assassins ceased to exist. But they had many imitators in later ages.

The Gunpowder Plot

Another famous terrorist group that sought to use assassination as a political tool formed in England in 1604. At that time, the medieval era was giving way to early modern times. The group had no formal name. It became identified with one of its leaders—Guy Fawkes. History also associates the group with the scheme it planned—the Gunpowder Plot.

Fawkes and other members of the group were Catholics. They correctly thought that English Protestants were persecuting them. To retaliate they decided to plunge the country into a state of terror and chaos. Fawkes had earlier been a soldier and had become an expert with explosives. At his suggestion, the conspirators rented a cellar below the building where Parliament met. Then they filled the cellar with tons of gunpowder. Fawkes' plan was to blow up the building on November 5, 1605. All members of Parliament, along with King James I, were scheduled to meet there that day.

The authorities discovered the plot, and Fawkes was arrested. He and other members of the group were tortured, tried, and executed. Since then the English have celebrated Bonfire Night. Fireworks and other ceremonies symbolically give thanks for the country's narrow escape from disaster.

Some later national leaders were not so fortunate, however. In the centuries that followed, assassination remained a potent weapon in terrorism's arsenal.

Guy Fawkes, a conspirator in the Gundpowder Plot, was arrested and brought before King James I. Fawkes was hanged for treason in January 1606.

STRANGLERS AND //////
BOMBERS RUN AMOK

The Assassins' nearly 200-year presence made them longer-lived than most terrorist groups in history. But they did not endure nearly as long as India's most famous terrorist organization. Its members were known as the Thuggees. The group first appeared in the 1200s, about the same time the Assassins met their demise. The last Thuggees were not eliminated until the late 1800s.

Strange Motives and Beliefs

The Thuggees' name came from an ancient Indian word for thief. Their name also gave rise to a common English word—thug.

Thuggees often attacked people who were traveling on lonely stretches of road.

A thug is most often defined as a gangsterlike person who uses violent tactics. This is exactly what the Thuggees regularly did.

They usually would hide near country roads. When a group of travelers came by, some Thuggees would emerge. They would pretend that they, too, were travelers. After gaining their victims' trust, the terrorists would suddenly turn on them. Each Thuggee would pull out a yellow scarf. Winding it around a victim's neck, he would mercilessly strangle him or her to death. Usually the attackers robbed the lifeless bodies.

As a secret network of groups that committed murder, the Thuggees were among the first crime families.

Robbery was not the Thuggees' main motive, however. Their brand of terrorism was driven by their extreme religious views. Like most Indians, the group's members were Hindus. Among the most popular Hindu deities was Kali, a goddess of both creation and destruction. Unlike other Hindus, the Thuggees believed that Kali demanded ritual killings. These violent acts were thought to preserve a strange, unexplained balance of life on Earth. So it appears that the Thuggees believed that their killings were not murders. Instead, they claimed, they were doing the goddess's bidding, and she would reward them in the afterlife.

Whatever the Thuggees' motives and beliefs were, there is no question that they spread terror far and wide. Modern experts think that the Thuggees killed tens of thousands of people over the centuries. The fear

The Thuggees in Popular Culture

The fear created by the Thuggees made them a frequent topic of popular media, including books and later movies. Particularly popular was the 1839 book *Confessions of a Thug*, by English novelist Philip M. Taylor. In the 20th century, interest in the Thuggees revived. Moviemakers began to portray the Thuggees' acts of murder and mayhem. For example they were the villains of the classic 1939 film *Gunga Din*, which was inspired by Rudyard Kipling's famous poem of the same name. The Thuggees also figured prominently in the films *Indiana Jones and the Temple of Doom* (1984) and *The Deceivers* (1988).

The British wanted to stop the Thuggees' reign of fear and violence.

and carnage they caused might have continued indefinitely. But the British military finally put a stop to it.

The British made India a colony in the 1800s. They were appalled by the threat to law and order posed by the Thuggees, and they launched a full-scale assault on the group. In the 1830s and 1840s, Captain William Sleeman arrested and executed many Thuggees. He also exposed their methods, which helped travelers avoid becoming victims. Because of these efforts, by the 1870s the Thuggees had ceased to exist.

Terror in Czarist Russia

Not long after the Thuggees were defeated in India, a frightening terrorist group arose in Russia. It was called Narodnaya Volya, meaning "People's Will." Its members chose bombs over knives or strangle cords as their main weapons.

Like the Assassins, members of People's Will turned to terror as a political tool. Before the early 1900s, Russia was led by absolute rulers called czars. Their word was law, and their policies were often undemocratic and sometimes harsh. As a result, many Russians felt oppressed and longed for a more just society. Some came to believe that a violent revolution was the only way to make things better.

In 1869 two Russian revolutionaries, Mikhail Bakunin and Sergei Nechayev, published a book titled *Catechism of Revolution*. In it they described revolutionaries: "The revolutionist is a doomed man. He has no private interests, no affairs,

Mikhail Bakunin spent time in prison and in a work camp in Siberia for his participation in the 1848 Czech rebellion.

sentiments, ties, property nor even a name of his own. His entire being is devoured by one purpose, one thought, one passion—the revolution. … He has severed every link with the social order and with the entire civilized world: with the laws, good manners, conventions, and morality of that world. He is its merciless enemy and continues to inhabit it with only one purpose—to destroy it."

The book inspired some Russians who wanted to see reforms instituted. In 1876 they formed an organization called Land and Liberty. It demanded that the czars give up their power and hand over government-owned land to poor farmers. No reforms began. In 1879 the group split into two sections. One, called Black Reparation, did not condone the use of terror. The other section—People's Will—did embrace such methods.

Members of People's Will first demanded that the government allow the creation of a citizen assembly. It would write a new constitution. That document would establish freedom of speech and freedom of the press, as well as oversee the redistribution of land to the poor. The group stated its demands in its own underground newspaper, *The Worker's Gazette*.

Next People's Will began the bombings for which it became famous. In early 1880, the group bombed a building in which Czar Alexander II was scheduled to have dinner. He was delayed, so he escaped death. But 67 people were killed.

The following year he was not as fortunate. On March 13, 1881, Czar Alexander II was killed by a bomb thrown by a member of People's Will. Most of the people who planned the attack were captured and hanged. Other members of the group remained at large. In March 1887, they tried to kill Alexander's son, Czar Alexander III, but they failed. In the months that followed, the czar's police arrested almost 2,000 members of People's Will. Some were imprisoned, and others were exiled.

People's Will soon fell apart. But its former members inspired a new generation of revolutionaries who looked up to the work of People's Will. The new revolutionaries' efforts led to the 1917 Russian Revolution, which overthrew the czarist government. This is an example of how a terrorist organization can continue to inspire violence long after it ceases to exist.

Czar Alexander II brought some reform to Russia during his reign, though not enough to satisfy everyone. After his assassination in March 1881, citizens lost many freedoms.

STRIKING AT //////////
NATIONAL SYMBOLS

The examples set by 19th century terrorist organizations like
People's Will inspired the growth of similar groups worldwide in
the 20th century. Some of the groups cited religious motives for
their violent acts. Even more had political goals. For instance the
Irish Republican Army wanted British rule in Ireland to end. So its
members staged assassinations and bombings against British targets.

In the Middle East, several terrorist groups formed in
opposition to Israel. One, the Popular Front for the Liberation of
Palestine, wanted to eliminate Israel and replace it with an Arab
state. To this end, the PFLP committed various violent acts. These
included hijacking airliners and bombing supermarkets.

A Palestinian terrorist appeared on the balcony of the Israeli
dormitory at the Olympic village in September 1972. The terrorists
killed two Israelis and kept nine more hostages, who later died.

Massacre at the Olympics

Another anti-Israeli Palestinian group, Black September, made bigger headlines than had the PFLP. It did so by imitating earlier terrorists who had struck at national symbols. Guy Fawkes and his colleagues had targeted Parliament. Members of People's Will had attacked the czars. Aiming at such high-profile targets had often proved a sure-fire way of gaining major publicity for one's cause.

With this in mind, the leaders of Black September plotted to disrupt the Olympic Games in Munich, Germany, in 1972. The Olympics is one of the biggest of all international events. The teams that take part are proud national symbols within their own countries. Black September targeted the Israeli national team.

On September 5, the terrorists sneaked into the Olympic Village, where about 8,000 athletes were lodged. The attackers barged into the quarters of the Israeli athletes. Wrestling coach Yossef Romano and weightlifter Moshe Weinberg fought back. This allowed several athletes to escape. Then the intruders shot and killed Romano and Weinberg and took nine others hostage.

As the world press zeroed in on the unfolding crisis, the terrorists made demands. They wanted the release of 200 Palestinian fighters held in Israeli jails. They also demanded to be flown in helicopters to the Munich airport and by jet to Cairo, Egypt.

The German authorities agreed to supply the helicopters and jet, but this was a ploy. When the terrorists and their hostages reached the airport, German commandos moved in and opened fire. In the commotion, all nine of the hostages were killed. So were a German policeman and five of the

Eleven members of the 1972 Israeli Olympic team died after their quarters in the Olympic Village were invaded by Palestinian terrorists.

terrorists. In the end, Black September had failed to achieve its goals. Still it had demonstrated to other terrorist groups that attacking high-profile targets was the best way to gain world attention.

Al-Qaida's Continuing Threat

No terrorist group has used this approach more effectively than al-Qaida. An Islamic extremist group originally based in Afghanistan, it rose to prominence in the 1990s. Its leader is Osama bin Laden. One of bin Laden's goals is to force Westerners and non-Muslims out of Muslim countries. His group also wants the formation of Islamic theocracies in the Middle East and elsewhere—national governments run by religious leaders who follow religious laws.

Hoping to achieve its goals, al-Qaida bombed two U.S. embassies in Africa in 1998. These were high-profile targets, but the attacks did not satisfy bin Laden. He was determined to take his fight directly to U.S. soil and strike at American national symbols.

The Rise of al-Qaida

Osama bin Laden, a founder of al-Qaida, was born in Saudi Arabia in 1957. In 1979 he went to Afghanistan. There he and other foreigners helped local Muslims fight the Soviets, who had recently invaded. Over time the Soviets suffered many setbacks. In 1989 they were forced to withdraw from Afghanistan. By that time bin Laden and others had established their own group of fighters, which became al-Qaida.

The members of the group were angry with the United States for stationing troops in Saudi Arabia. Bin Laden strongly opposes the presence of U.S. troops in Muslim countries. He and his followers vowed to punish the United States and other Western countries. In August 1998, al-Qaida bombed U.S. embassies in the African countries of Tanzania and Kenya. The blasts killed more than 220 people and injured about 5,000. These violent acts gave al-Qaida members what they wanted—worldwide attention.

The operation he and his lieutenants had in mind took years of careful planning. Part of the scheme involved sending several al-Qaida members to live and work undercover in the United States.

At least 60 people were killed and more than 1,000 were injured in August 1998, when a bomb exploded near the U.S. Embassy and a bank in Nairobi, Kenya.

The plan was carried out September 11, 2001. Nineteen Islamic extremists, most of them Saudis, hijacked four U.S. commercial airliners. Flying the planes themselves, the terrorists used them as weapons. They crashed one into the North Tower of the World Trade Center in New York City. Minutes later a second plane struck the South Tower. A third hijacked plane smashed into the Pentagon, near Washington, D.C. The plan called for crashing the fourth plane into either the White House or the U.S. Capitol. But the passengers fought back. As a result, the aircraft crashed in a field in Pennsylvania, killing all on board.

Soon the burning and mangled World Trade Center towers collapsed. Nearly 3,000 people died there, at the Pentagon, and in the crash in Pennsylvania. Bin Laden had achieved his goal of getting global attention by striking at U.S. national symbols. Al-Qaida became one of the most notorious terrorist groups in history. It also became the most hunted. Soon after the September 11 attacks, the United States invaded Afghanistan and drove out al-Qaida and its chief supporters.

Bin Laden eventually took refuge in a remote, mountainous area of Pakistan. His organization, which had for a while been in disarray, had regained its former strength. Nations in the 21st century appear to be no less vulnerable than nations in earlier times to the threat of terrorist groups.

Many people who survived the September 11 attacks later suffered effects from breathing the dust and ash from the Twin Towers' collapse.

THE THREAT OF ///////// DOMESTIC TERROR

When most Americans hear the word *terrorist*, they probably think of Middle Easterners or other foreigners. The idea that Americans commit terrorist acts rarely comes to mind. Yet many terrible acts have been carried out in America by U.S. citizens. Experts refer to this brand of violence as domestic terrorism or home-grown terrorism.

The Ku Klux Klan

The most famous and longest-lived American terrorist organization is the original Ku Klux Klan. The KKK was established in the mid-1860s, right after the end of the Civil

KKK members usually wore white hoods and long robes to disguise their identities.

War. When the U.S. government freed all black slaves, some whites, especially in the South, were upset. They did not like the idea of African-Americans' having the same rights as whites. In particular they resented that blacks could vote and run for public office.

The Klan was created in response to these supposed threats to traditional, white-controlled society. As time went on, KKK members used threats and violence to instill fear into black people. Typical tactics included beatings and, in some cases, murders. Hanging victims from trees became common, although some victims were shot or beaten to death. A terror tactic the Klan adopted later, in the early 20th century, was burning large wooden crosses at night. Often the fires were meant to warn potential KKK targets.

The Klan's chief goals were to maintain a white-controlled society and to keep blacks from voting. But the KKK also expressed hatred for other minorities. These included Jews, Catholics, and several immigrant groups.

After a while, the original KKK lost many members, as well as much of its social influence. This was partly because the U.S. government officially labeled it a terrorist group in 1870. In 1915, however, a new and more popular version of the Klan emerged. It reached the height of its power in the mid-1920s, when it boasted as many as 4 million members. But its popularity was short-lived. In the late 1920s, newspaper editorials across the country called the KKK un-American. Many local authorities cracked down on the group's terrorist activities. By 1930 its membership was down to about 30,000.

In the following decades, many smaller groups formed, each identifying itself as either the Klan or

KKK members often burned crosses at meetings and on the lawns of people they hoped to scare.

a chapter of the organization. Some of the groups committed murders and other violent acts in the 1950s and 1960s in an effort to stop the civil rights movement. These efforts failed, and the KKK continued to shrink.

Today it has about 8,000 members in about 150 chapters. Most Americans view the Klan as a despicable hate group. Law enforcement authorities, including the FBI, keep a close watch on its activities.

Lone Terrorists

Unlike the members of the KKK, some American domestic terrorists have acted alone rather than in groups. One of the most famous is Theodore Kaczynski, better known as the Unabomber. A former college professor, he turned to violence in order to call attention to the ongoing destruction of the environment by industry and technology. From 1978 to 1995, he sent 16 bombs through the mail. The resulting explosions killed three people and injured 23.

The death toll created by another lone terrorist, Timothy McVeigh, was much larger. Born in 1968, McVeigh grew up to be a troubled young man. He became fascinated by guns as a child. He sometimes carried hidden guns to school, hoping to impress other students. As time went on, McVeigh came to view the U.S. government as corrupt and dangerous.

Timothy McVeigh said he was bullied as a child and dreamed of getting even.

In 1992 he wrote a letter to a newspaper in Buffalo, New York: "Taxes are a joke. Regardless of what a political candidate 'promises,' they will increase. [The politicians] mess up. We suffer. ... [They] are out of control. ... What is it going to take to open the eyes of our elected officials? America is in serious decline! ... Is a Civil War imminent? Do we have to shed blood to reform the current system?"

McVeigh learned how to make explosives. Early in 1995 he told a friend that the people running the government were guilty of treason and needed to be punished.

On April 19, 1995, McVeigh carried out the worst domestic terrorist act in U.S. history. He packed explosives into a truck. Then he parked it in front of the Alfred P. Murrah Federal Building in Oklahoma City. The enormous blast from the explosives tore the walls off one side of the building. The dead numbered 168, including 19 children. Nearly 700 people were injured.

The Oklahoma City National Memorial includes 168 empty chairs, which respresent those who died in the explosion.

McVeigh was arrested soon after the disaster. During his trial, he expressed no remorse for the killings. Convicted of 11 federal offenses, including first-degree murder, McVeigh was executed by lethal injection on June 11, 2001.

Another lone domestic terrorist struck a few months later. He became known as the "anthrax killer." Beginning September 18, he sent letters to news media offices and the offices of two U.S. senators. The letters contained tiny pieces of the deadly substance anthrax. A person who opened a letter and inhaled the spores was in danger of contracting the illness. Twenty-two people were infected. Five of them died.

Because the September 11 attacks had occurred only a week earlier, many Americans at first feared that al-Qaida had sent the letters. But it later became clear that the culprit was an American. In July 2008, the FBI zeroed in on Dr. Bruce Ivins, a scientist working for the U.S. Army. Just before he was formally charged with the crimes, he committed suicide. Ivins was against abortion, and some people believe he may have wanted to harm senators and other officials who supported abortion rights.

A Part of History

No one knows when or where the next terrorist attack will occur. It might happen in the United States. Or it might occur somewhere else in the world. On the bright side, many governments around the world have strengthened safety measures. These have made it much more difficult for terrorist plots to succeed. Unfortunately, however, experts expect that on occasion, some terrorists will be successful. The sad fact is that terrorism has always been a part of human history, and this unpleasant reality is not likely to change anytime soon.

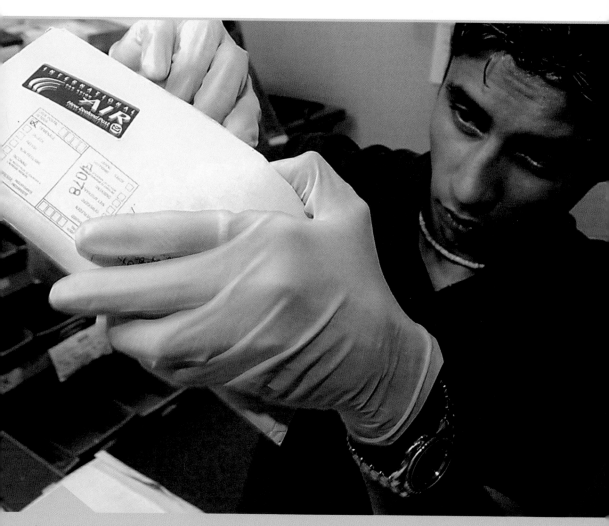

After anthrax was found in envelopes in the United States, people around the world took extra precautions when handling mail.

Timeline

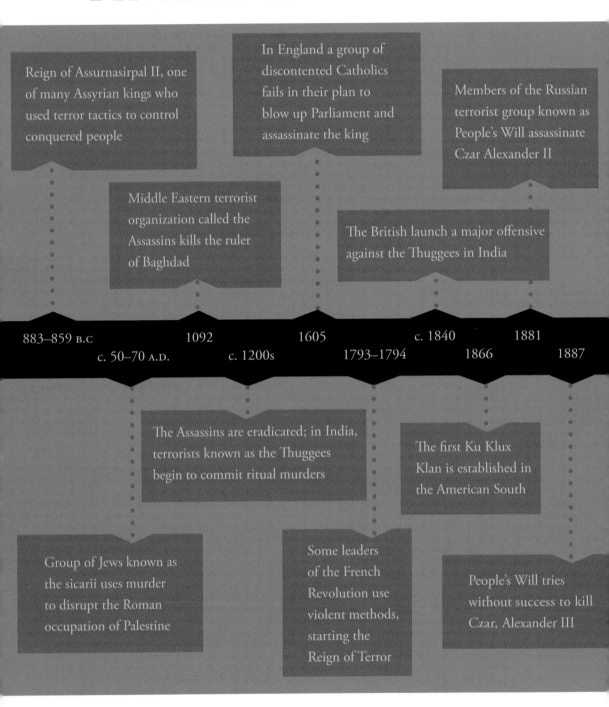

Reign of Assurnasirpal II, one of many Assyrian kings who used terror tactics to control conquered people

In England a group of discontented Catholics fails in their plan to blow up Parliament and assassinate the king

Members of the Russian terrorist group known as People's Will assassinate Czar Alexander II

Middle Eastern terrorist organization called the Assassins kills the ruler of Baghdad

The British launch a major offensive against the Thuggees in India

883–859 B.C   1092   1605   c. 1840   1881

c. 50–70 A.D.   c. 1200s   1793–1794   1866   1887

The Assassins are eradicated; in India, terrorists known as the Thuggees begin to commit ritual murders

The first Ku Klux Klan is established in the American South

Group of Jews known as the sicarii uses murder to disrupt the Roman occupation of Palestine

Some leaders of the French Revolution use violent methods, starting the Reign of Terror

People's Will tries without success to kill Czar, Alexander III

Black September, a Palestinian terrorist group, attacks Israeli athletes at the Olympic Games in Munich, Germany

On September 11, hijacked planes flown by members of al-Qaida crash into the World Trade Center towers, the Pentagon, and a field in Pennsylvania; the "anthrax killer" strikes, killing five

KKK membership reaches about 4 million

American domestic terrorist Timothy McVeigh bombs a federal building in Oklahoma City, killing 168 people

Osama bin Laden and several followers remain at large in the border areas of Afghanistan and Pakistan

1920s

1939

1972

1991

1995

1998

2001

2008

2009

The movie *Gunga Din* portrays the conflict between the British and Thuggees

The U.S. military presence in Saudi Arabia angers Osama bin Laden and his al-Qaida followers, who pledge revenge against the United States, Saudi Arabia, and other Middle Eastern governments

Dr. Bruce Ivins, the FBI's suspect in the anthrax killings, commits suicide

Al-Qaida bombs two U.S. embassies in Africa, killing more than 200 people

GLOSSARY

anthrax—deadly disease spread by tiny seedlike particles called spores

assassination—murder of someone who is well known or important, often for political reasons

carnage—killing of many people

cell—subgroup of a larger organization

commandos—members of a raiding expedition

conspirator—someone who takes part in a plot to commit a crime

deity—god or goddess

invincible—unable to be defeated

lethal injection—method of execution in which deadly chemicals are injected into a prisoner's body

Parliament—England's national lawmaking body

remorse—feelings of guilt and regret after doing something wrong

retaliate—to strike back

stronghold—place that is well protected against attack

terrorism—use of violence to kill, injure, or create fear, often for political reasons

theocracy—government run by religious leaders

Additional Resources

Further Reading

Englar, Mary. *September 11*. Minneapolis: Compass Point Books, 2007.

Klobuchar, Lisa. *1963 Birmingham Church Bombing: The Ku Klux Klan's History of Terror*. Minneapolis: Compass Point Books, 2009.

Landau, Elaine. *Suicide Bombers: Foot Soldiers of the Terrorist Movement*. Minneapolis: Twenty-First Century Books, 2007.

Langley, Andrew. *September 11: Attack on America*. Minneapolis: Compass Point Books, 2006.

Levin, Jack. *Domestic Terrorism*. New York: Chelsea House, 2006.

Moghadam, Assaf. *The Roots of Terrorism*. New York: Chelsea House Publishers, 2006.

Internet Sites

FactHound offers a safe, fun way to find Internet sites related to this book. All of the sites on FactHound have been researched by our staff.

Here's all you do:
Visit *www.facthound.com*
FactHound will fetch the best sites for you!

Look for other books in this series:

Combating Terrorism
Terrorist Groups
What Makes a Terrorist?

Select Bibliography

Archer, Christon I., et al. *World History of Warfare*. Lincoln: University of Nebraska Press, 2002.

Bailey, Brian. *Massacres: An Account of Crimes Against Humanity*. London: Orion, 1994.

Chaliand, Gérard, and Arnaud Blin, eds. *The History of Terrorism: From Antiquity to Al Qaeda*. Berkeley: University of California Press, 2007.

Combs, Cindy C. *Terrorism in the Twenty-first Century*. New York: Pearson/Longman, 2009.

Combs, Cindy C., and Martin Slann. *Encyclopedia of Terrorism*. New York: Facts on File, 2007.

Friedman, Thomas L. *Longitudes and Latitudes: The World in the Age of Terrorism*. New York: Anchor Books, 2003.

Haught, James A. *Holy Horrors: An Illustrated History of Religious Murder and Madness*. Amherst, N.Y.: Prometheus Books, 2002.

Lewis, Bernard. *The Assassins: A Radical Sect in Islam*. New York: Basic Books, 2003.

McNeill, William H. *The Pursuit of Power: Technology, Armed Force, and Society Since A.D. 1000*. Chicago: University of Chicago Press, 1982.

Richardson, Louise, ed. *The Roots of Terrorism*. New York: Routledge, 2006.

Turchie, Terry D., and Kathleen M. Puckett. *Hunting the American Terrorist: The FBI's War on Homegrown Terror*. Palisades, N.Y.: History Pub. Co., 2007.

Wagner, Kim A. *Thuggee: Banditry and the British in Early Nineteenth-Century India*. Basingstoke, England: Palgrave Macmillan, 2007.

Index

About the Author

Historian and award-winning writer Don Nardo has written numerous books for young readers about the ancient, medieval, and modern worlds. These include overviews of the civilizations of ancient Mesopotamia, Greece, and Rome; medieval castles, weapons, and feudalism; the French Revolution; the early United States and its founding documents; America's wars; and a four-volume study of the Industrial Revolution in Britain and America. Nardo lives with his wife, Christine, in Massachusetts.